Drawing Collection by Modern Artists

CONTENTS

Albert Gleizes, 1881~1953

Albert Gleizes was born on December 8, 1881, in Paris, France. His father was an industrial designer and owner of a textile factory, which allowed Gleizes to learn about the techniques and craftsmanship involved in textile manufacturing from a young age. He had little interest in his school studies, instead developing a deep fascination for art and literature, often skipping classes to write poetry or wander the neighborhood in search of inspiration. In his youth, he decided to pursue a career as a painter, working in a post-Impressionist style and soon embracing the ideals and principles of Fauvism, creating modern and innovative works through geometric simplification.

In the 1910s, he became deeply immersed in the Cubist movement and, alongside French painter and art theorist Jean Metzinger, published the book "Du Cubisme," establishing himself as a key theorist of Cubism. Later, Gleizes shifted his focus to religious themes, beginning to create murals and experimenting with the combination of traditional Catholic themes and Cubism as he entered his later years. This approach brought a refreshing shock to the contemporary art scene.

In the 1930s, he concentrated on art education and writing, passing on Cubism and his artistic philosophy to young artists. He continued to produce work during World War II, and after the war, he returned to Paris and resumed his active artistic career. In 1947, he published "Life and Death," a book systematically explaining the principles and philosophy of Cubist painting.

He passed away on June 23, 1953, in Sérignan-du-Comtat, near Avignon, France. Gleizes is regarded as a major theorist and practitioner of Cubism, known for his innovative approach that combined art and theory, marking him as an important figure in modern art.

Houses in a Valley, 1910

31 x 23.9 cm

Landscape with Bridge and Viaduct, 1910

Two Women Seated by a Window, 1914

André Derain, 1880~1954

André Derain is known as a French painter, sculptor, stage designer, and one of the founders of Fauvism. In 1905, he collaborated with Henri Émile Benoît Matisse to showcase vibrant Fauvist works characterized by intense colors and forms. Initially, he gained fame for his landscape paintings in the Fauvist style, but he continued to seek new stylistic developments throughout his career.

Derain was a pioneer in collecting African art, and his early works prominently reflect the influences of Cubism and African art. He later developed a deep interest in archaeological artifacts and Renaissance painting, gradually showing a tendency to return to more traditional styles over time.

In 1931, a collection of critiques titled "Defend or Reject André Derain" was published, reflecting the mixed evaluations of his work. There was ongoing controversy regarding the increasingly conservative tone of his pieces. Supporters viewed his evolution positively and criticized modernism, while detractors harshly claimed that his new works were contemplative and mechanical. Despite this debate, Derain continued to achieve success, with his work consistently receiving significant attention. In 1935, he held a retrospective in Bern, and in 1937, he exhibited at the Salon d'Automne in Paris, showcasing his accomplishments to many.

However, with the outbreak of World War II, he faced challenges, including accusations of collaboration with the Third Reich, divorce, and personal crises, leading him into a state of self-doubt. Tragically, he died in 1954 after being struck by a truck.

Throughout his life, Derain sought to balance Fauvism and traditional art forms. His work continues to inspire future artists and is regarded as an important resource for those exploring artistic creativity to this day.

49 x 64 cm

Still Life with Apples, 1921

33 x 22 cm

Arshile Gorky, 1904~1948

Arshile Gorky was born in 1904 in a small village in Turkey (then Armenia). His father immigrated to the United States in 1910 to escape military conscription, and when Turkey invaded Armenia in 1915, Gorky fled with his mother and sister. In 1919, his mother died of starvation, and a year later, Gorky crossed to America and settled in New England at the age of just sixteen. The tragedies and hardships he experienced in his childhood would later become central themes in his work.

Gorky began studying art at the Design New School in Boston and moved to New York in 1925 to continue his studies. He frequently visited art museums in New York, where he was influenced by modern European artists such as Paul Cézanne, Pablo Ruiz Picasso, Georges Braque, and Joan Miró. Gorky's transition from Cubism to Surrealism began to attract the attention of critics.

Starting in the 1930s, Gorky gradually began to showcase his work to the public. In 1934, he held his first solo exhibition at the Mellon Gallery in Philadelphia, and from 1935 to 1939, he participated in the Works Progress Administration (WPA) Federal Art Project, creating murals. By the 1940s, he gained recognition from major art museums in New York, establishing himself as an artist. Beginning in 1945, his works, featuring floating organic forms that intertwined to create almost abstract landscapes, began to receive public acclaim. However, he continued to face hardships. In 1946, a fire in his Connecticut studio destroyed about 30 of his works, and a month later, he was diagnosed with cancer and underwent surgery. These setbacks contributed to his struggle with depression. In 1947, he suffered a broken neck in a car accident, and his wife left him, taking their two children. After that, Gorky committed suicide in his studio in July 1948.

Leonora Portnoff, 1935

32 x 24.3 cm

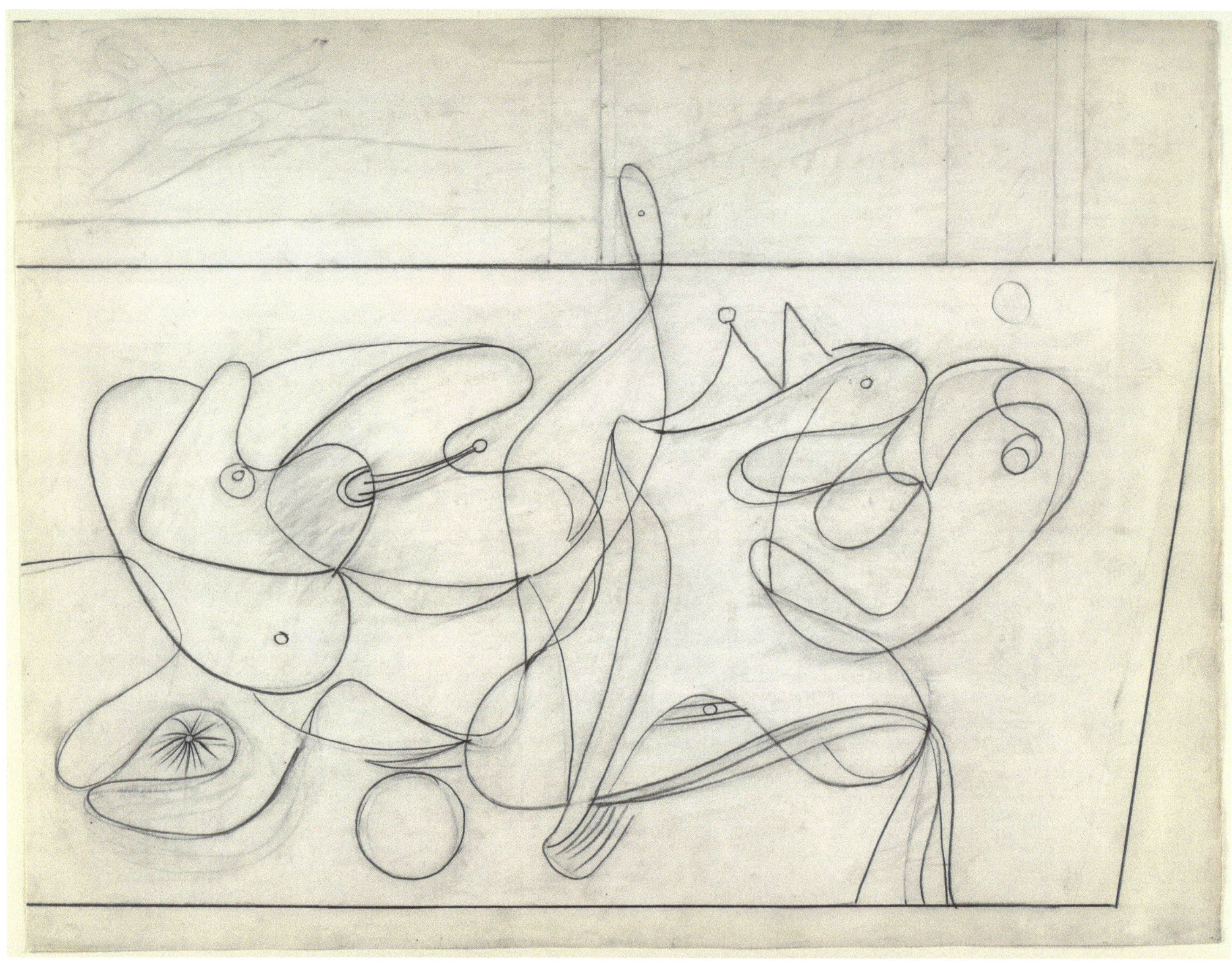

Accademia Gallery, Florence, Italy

55.9 x 76.2 cm

Claude Monet, 1840~1926

Claude Monet was a master of French Impressionism, and the term "Impressionism" originated from his work Impression, Sunrise (1872). Monet was born in Paris and spent his childhood in the port city of Le Havre, where he developed an interest in art. Around the age of 18, he met a pivotal figure in his life, Eugène Boudin, who was a French landscape painter known for his outdoor painting. Monet learned the fundamentals of painting from Boudin, who encouraged him to closely observe and depict landscapes outdoors. During this time, he also became acquainted with the Dutch landscape painter Johan Barthold Jongkind, from whom he learned techniques for capturing light in the atmosphere, which would greatly assist him in establishing his Impressionist style later on.

In 1859, at the age of 19, Monet moved to Paris and interacted with Camille Pissarro at the Académie Suisse. In 1860, he was drafted into the military but was discharged in 1862 due to contracting typhus. After his discharge, he joined Charles Gleyre's studio, where he befriended Pierre-Auguste Renoir, Alfred Sisley, and Jean Frédéric Bazille. In 1870, he married his lover and model, Camille-Léonie Doncieux, and moved to London due to the Franco-Prussian War. In London, he encountered the works of British landscape painters such as Joseph Mallord William Turner and John Constable, which greatly inspired him with their vibrant and vivid colors.

In 1873, Monet helped organize an anonymous artists' group composed of painters, engravers, and sculptors, which became the foundation of Impressionism. In 1874, he exhibited Impression, Sunrise at their first group exhibition. The critic Louis Leroy mockingly described the work as "truly impressive," and this comment led to the group of painters, centered around Monet, being labeled as "Impressionists."

Monet firmly established his position as a leader of the group by exhibiting many works at the eight Impressionist exhibitions held until 1886, contributing to the movement's growth. He adhered to the Impressionist principle that "there are no inherent colors in objects; colors change according to light." By repeatedly painting the same subject from different perspectives and at different times, he captured the changes in light and color on canvas. In 1883, he purchased a farmhouse in Giverny, about 100 kilometers from Paris, where he created a garden with a pond and spent the rest of his life. Although he suffered from cataracts in his later years and could not see well, he continued to depict the ever-changing landscape of the pond and water lilies until his death.

Monet passed away in 1926 at the age of 86 from lung cancer and was buried in a church in Giverny. His house was donated to the French Academy of Arts and has since become the Monet Museum, a popular tourist destination.

24.6 x 33.4 cm

El Lissitzky, 1890~1941

El Lissitzky was a Russian avant-garde artist active in the early 20th century, known for his innovative works across various fields. Born on November 11, 1890, in Pochinok, a Jewish community in Russia, he recognized his artistic talent during his childhood in Vitebsk and Smolensk. At the age of 13, he began studying art under painter Yehuda Pen and even taught other students.

After failing to gain admission to an art academy, Lissitzky moved to Germany to study architectural engineering. During this time, he traveled throughout Europe, drawing artistic inspiration. In 1914, he returned to Russia, achieving success in the field of architecture. Later, at the invitation of Marc Chagall, he returned to Vitebsk, where he worked at the People's Art School, teaching various art disciplines.

Lissitzky devised a new painting style called Proun and, along with Kazimir Malevich, co-founded the supremacist artist group UNOVIS, establishing himself as a key figure in Russian avant-garde art. His work, particularly Beat the Whites with the Red Wedge (1919), captured the spirit of the Russian Revolution and garnered significant attention. He developed a personal artistic language called "Proun," which combined elements of Futurism and Constructivism into an innovative style.

Lissitzky gained recognition in the art centers of Europe and showcased his revolutionary art and design in various locations, including Germany and the Netherlands. Upon returning to Moscow, he worked at the Vkhutemas (State Higher Artistic and Technical Workshops), where he taught interior design and architecture. He also researched typography and photomontage, contributing to advancements in these fields.

Study for a page of the book Of Two Squares A Suprematist Tale in Six Constructions, 1920

25 x 21 cm

Félix Del Marle, 1889~1952

Félix Del Marle was a French painter and sculptor who primarily contributed to the Futurist and Dada movements. Born in 1889 in Pont-sur-Sambre, France, he moved to Paris at the age of 18 to pursue art more seriously, studying at the Julien Academy where he encountered various artistic movements.

In the early 1910s, he became acquainted with Italian Futurism and actively participated in the movement after meeting its founder, Filippo Tommaso Marinetti. He reflected the mechanical aesthetics, speed, and celebration of urbanization associated with Futurism in his works. Notably, in 1914, he presented his artwork at the first major Futurist exhibition.

After the outbreak of World War I, Del Marle's work began to show the influence of Dadaism. Experiencing the destruction and chaos of the war, he resonated with Dada's radical rejection of existing artistic norms. He engaged in various avant-garde activities alongside the Dadaist group and, particularly in the early 1920s, interacted with several Dada artists while working in Berlin, Germany.

As the 1930s approached, he developed an interest in Surrealism and abstract art, exploring new media and techniques, and experimenting with various forms of artwork, including sculpture and installation art.

Looping, 1914

62.4 x 47.5 cm

Henri Emile Benoit Matisse, 1869~1954

Henri Matisse was a renowned French painter known for his contributions to various art forms, including sculpture and paper cutting. He was born in Le Cateau-Cambrésis, France. In his late teens, while working as a lawyer's assistant, he began taking drawing classes. After undergoing an appendectomy, he immersed himself in art, and following his mother's advice, he enrolled at the École des Beaux-Arts in Paris, where he studied under the Symbolist painter Gustave Moreau.

Influenced by French Impressionism, Matisse created his own distinctive works characterized by an obsession with color and form. His art left a strong impression on viewers through its unique compositions and vibrant color combinations. While his early works featured darker tones, after a summer vacation in Brittany, his palette transformed to reflect vivid colors and the play of natural light. Later, influenced by Fauvism, he experimented with various painting styles and techniques of light. His collaboration with André Derain further invigorated and intensified his work.

In addition to his success as a painter, Matisse excelled in design, particularly in curtain and stained glass designs, which gained significant acclaim. He remained active as a leading artist in France, with his work recognized worldwide. Matisse gained prominence among a group of painters known as the "Fauves," and his friendship with Pablo Picasso is well-known. Through his relationship with Sergei Shchukin, he also introduced his work to Russia and received the French Legion of Honor.

In 1940, after being diagnosed with duodenal cancer, Matisse continued to paint even after surgery, shifting to a new medium he called "cut-outs," where he used scissors instead of a brush, creating a fresh form of art.

à John Rewald
Henri Matisse 8/42

73 x 58.4 cm

39.7 x 52.1 cm

Henri Matisse 2/38

55 x 44 cm

26.6 x 21.9 cm

69.8 x 46 cm

The Plumed Hat 1

Henri-Matisse août 1914

John Marin, 1870~1953

John Marin was born in 1870 in Rutherford, New Jersey. Initially trained in architecture, he later studied painting in New York and Philadelphia. In 1905, while living in Paris, he was influenced by Impressionist painters such as James Abbott McNeill Whistler and Paul Cézanne. Eventually, he combined the colors of Fauvism with the compositional techniques of Cubism and Futurism to develop his own unique style.

Marin had a deep interest in landscapes and urban scenes, particularly focusing on the cityscapes of New York, which became a central theme in his work. He effectively captured the complexity and movement of the city, leaving a strong impression on viewers. By blending elements of Modernism and Impressionism, he formed an innovative and original style characterized by vibrant colors and bold lines. His solo exhibition at Alfred Stieglitz's gallery "291" in 1909, along with his participation in the Armory Show in 1913, garnered him attention in the American art scene.

From 1914 onward, he primarily depicted urban landscapes and the coast of Maine in watercolor. His use of transparent colors vividly conveyed the dynamic nature of the city and the coastline, showcasing his clarity of color and rapid brushwork.

Marin actively participated in the American Modernism movement, contributing to the cultivation of modern art rooted in American soil. His works expressed the landscapes of urban and coastal areas from a modern perspective, playing a significant role in the artistic development of the United States. His art is regarded as representative of American identity and artistic creativity.

Buoy, Maine, 1931

37.5 x 48.9 cm

Lower Manhattan, 1920

55.4 x 68 cm

54.5 x 67.5 cm

39 x 53 cm

Juan Gris(Juan José Victoriano González-Pérez), 1887~1927

Juan Gris was born on March 23, 1887, in Madrid, Spain. He primarily worked in France and is regarded as an important painter of the Modernist and Cubist movements.

In his youth, he left Spain and moved to Paris in 1906. In Paris, he was influenced by and collaborated with artists such as Pablo Picasso, Georges Braque, André Derain, and Albert Gleizes. He actively participated in Cubist-related work, and his pieces exhibited a unique style that explored and combined the principles of Cubism.

Gris's work is centered around the principles of synthetic Cubism, addressing subjects from various angles through the combination of color and form. His experiments in Cubism, integrating diverse colors and shapes, led to the creation of a new form of Cubism.

One of the most interesting aspects of his paintings is the presence of musical rhythms and literary themes that go beyond visual expression. His works visually convey the beats, harmonies, and rhythms of music, delivering a distinct sensory experience. He incorporated musical motifs, such as sheet music and instruments, into his art, and often addressed narrative or poetic themes inspired by literature.

Juan Gris passed away suddenly in Paris on May 11, 1927. Although he lived a short life, he remains one of the artists whose work continues to influence modern art today.

Breakfast, 1914

80 x 59 cm

Glass and Bottle, c.1913

46.3 x 31.1 cm

Juan Gris 1919.

Julio González, 1876~1942

Julio González was a sculptor and painter born in Barcelona, Spain. He learned metalworking techniques from his father, who was a metal craftsman, from a young age. After his father's passing, the González family moved to Paris. There, he interacted with various artists and developed an innovative approach to metal sculpture, exploring new interpretations of form and space.

In the early 1900s, González frequented the famous Barcelona art café Els Quatre Gats, where he met Picasso for the first time. During this period, his childhood experience with metalworking began to manifest in his art, giving his works a unique aesthetic and sophisticated geometric forms. In 1907, he made his debut in the Paris art scene by exhibiting six paintings at the Salon d'Automne. After the mid-1930s, his works gained recognition among American collectors and critics.

The repoussé technique, along with his use of iron sculpture and welding, was considered innovative and original at the time, earning him significant attention in the art world.

1938
1938
15-4
-1-
-3-

Study for Head 1

Study for Head 2

Study for Head 3

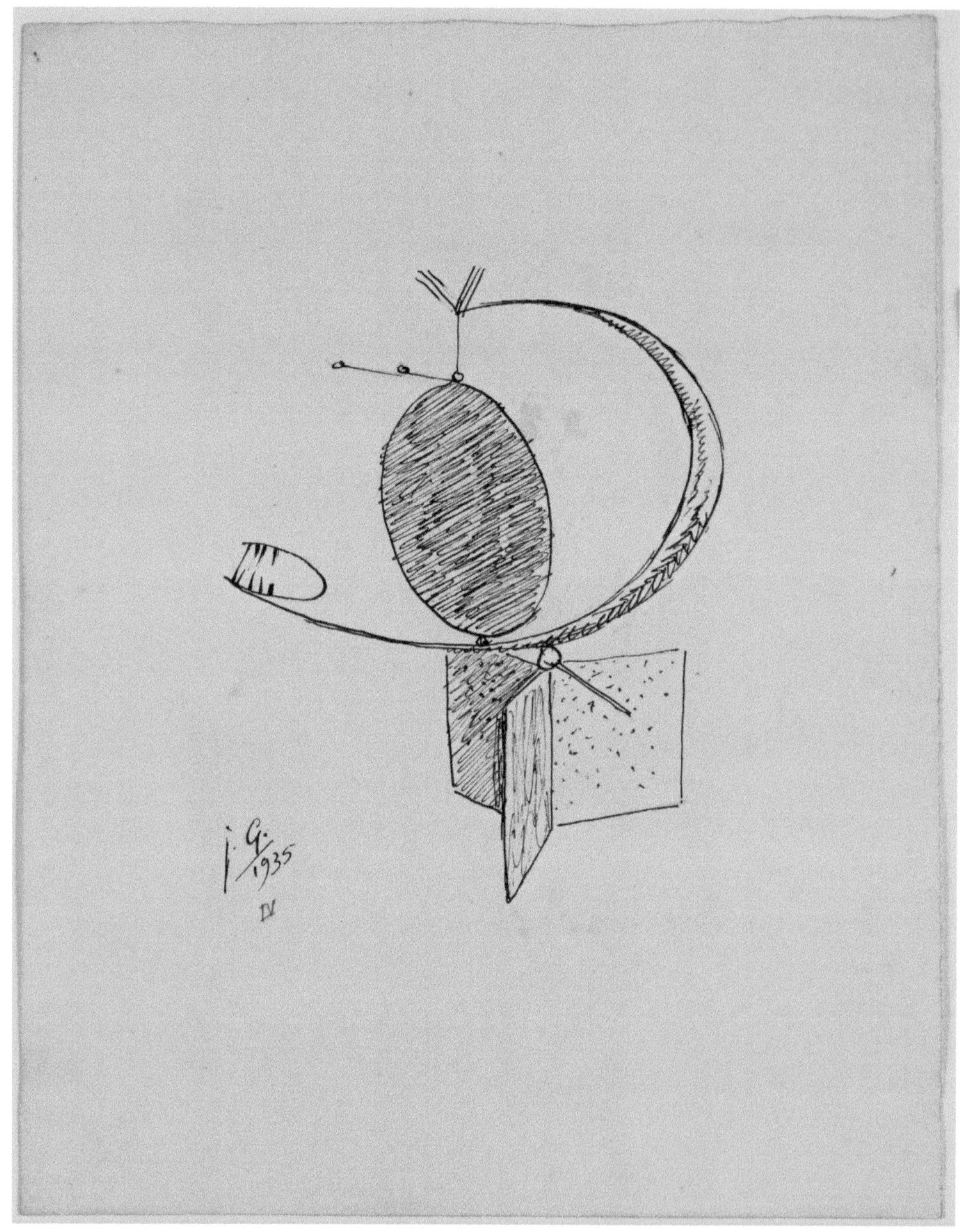

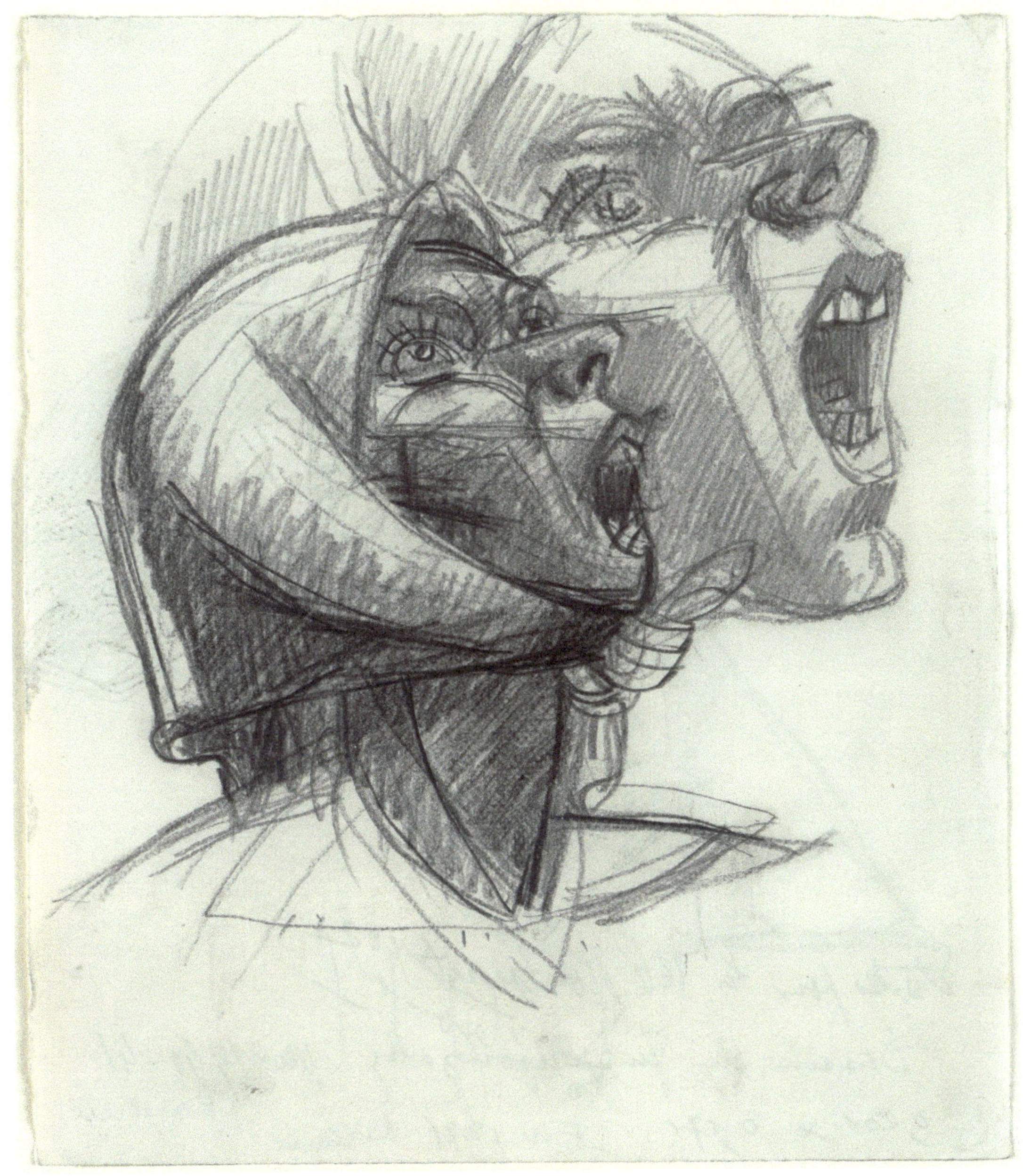

Study for Sculpture 1

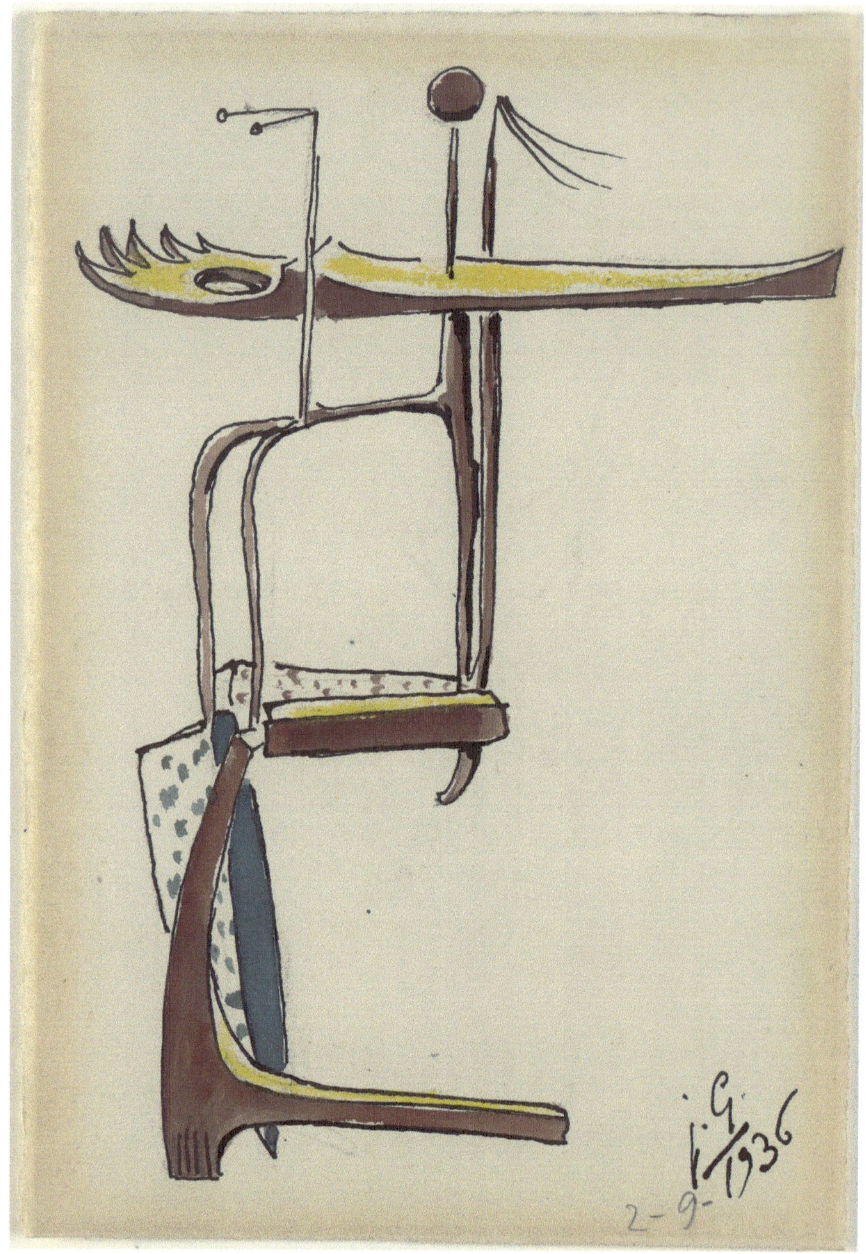

Study for Sculpture 2

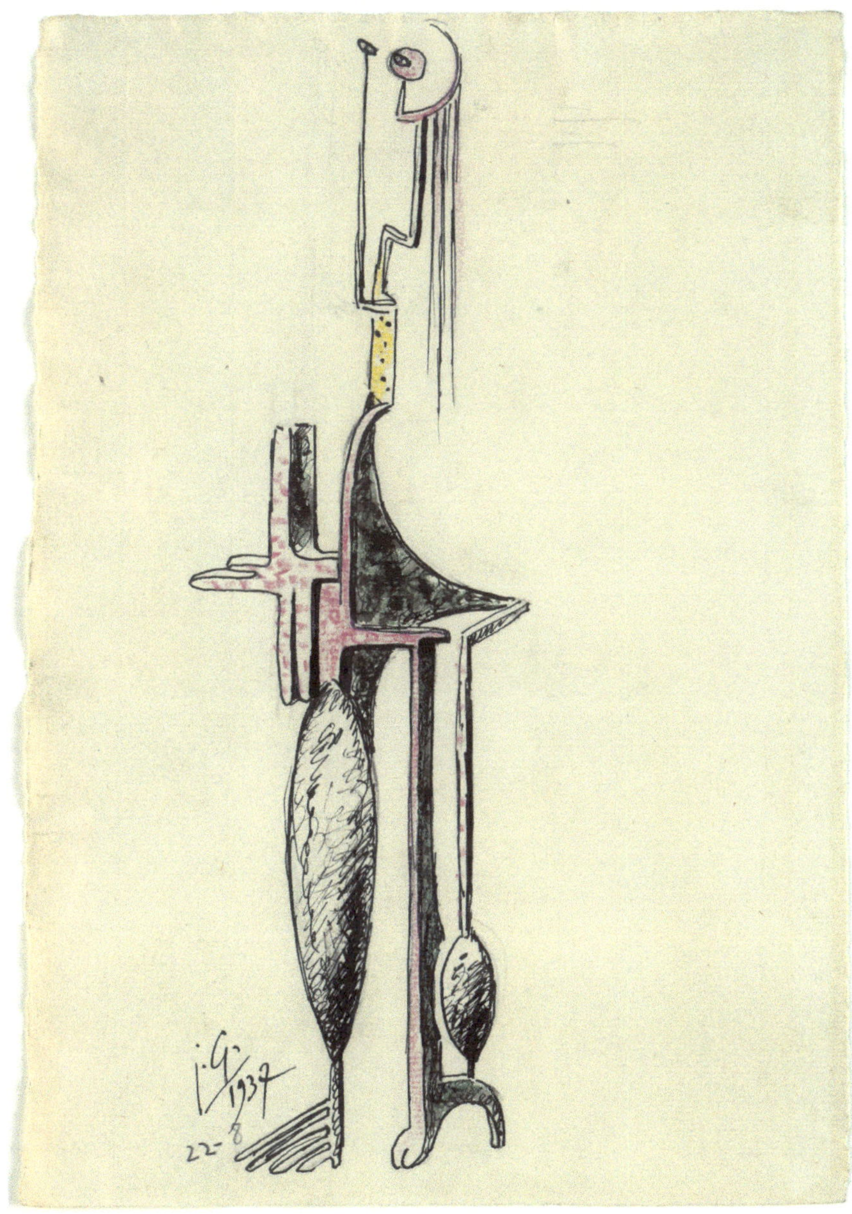

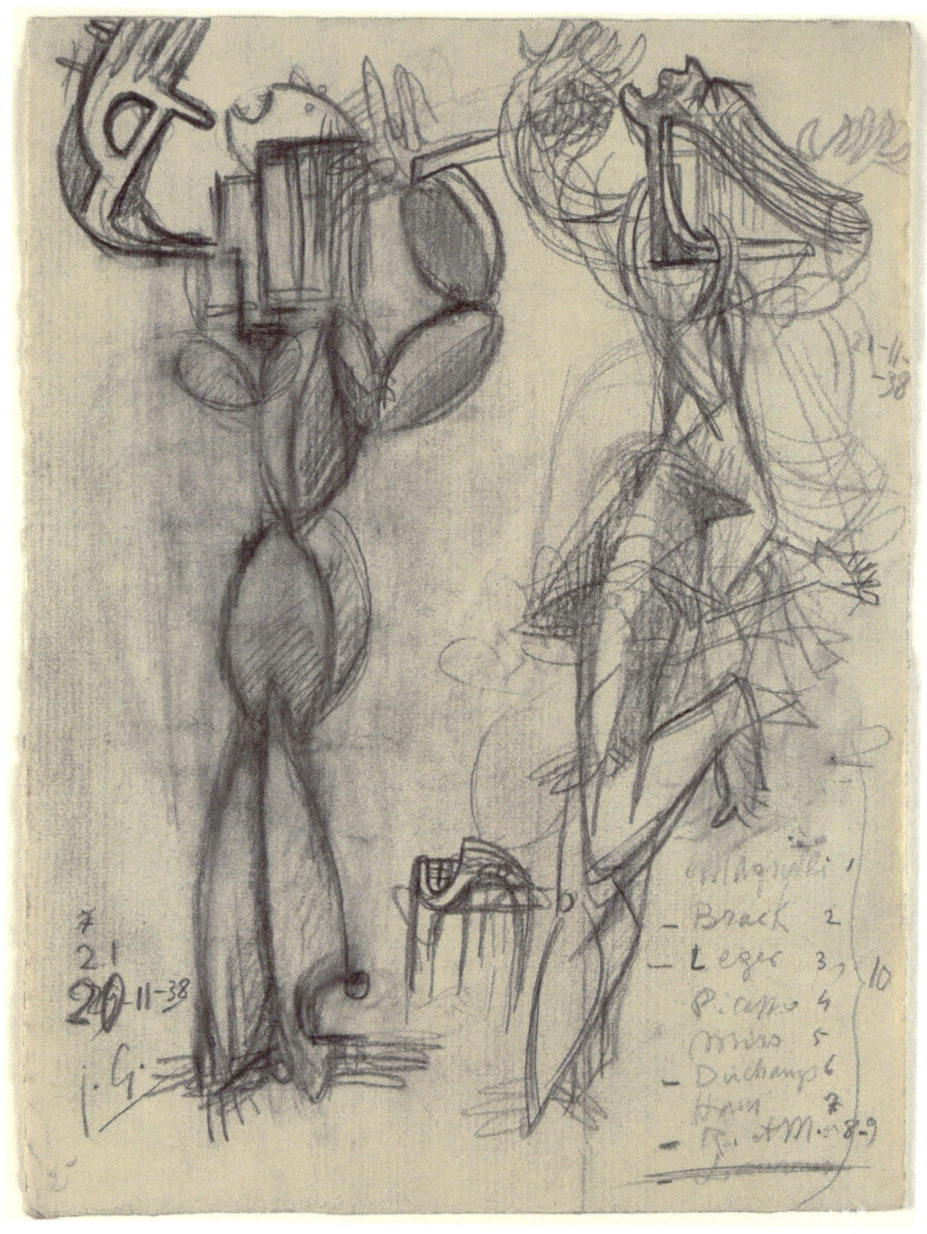
21-11-38
Brack 2
Leger 3
Picasso 4
Miro 5
Duchamp 6
10

Kazimir Malevich, 1879~1935

Kazimir Malevich was an innovative Russian painter and a pioneer of abstract art in the early 20th century, widely known as the founder of the Suprematism movement.

Born in 1878 to Polish parents in a small village near Kyiv, Ukraine, Malevich grew up with a passion for art, drawing landscapes of nature and everyday life. In 1896, his family moved to Kursk, Russia, where he began formal art education. By 1904, he had relocated to Moscow to study at the Moscow School of Painting, Sculpture and Architecture while also working in Fedor Rerberg's studio.

Initially influenced by Impressionism and Post-Impressionism, Malevich's early works evolved into various styles, including Symbolism and Art Nouveau. In the early 1910s, he underwent a radical stylistic transformation under the influences of Futurism and Cubism, leading to more geometric and abstract forms in his art.

In 1915, he exhibited his Suprematist works at the "Last Futurist Exhibition" in Saint Petersburg, where he unveiled his most famous piece, Black Square (1915). This shocking abstraction featured a simple black square on a canvas, through which Malevich aimed to explore the essential elements of art, revealing his deep interest in the purity of form and color. Suprematism sought to express emotion and spirituality through pure geometric shapes and colors, asserting that art could be an independent means of expression beyond mere imitation of reality. His theories significantly impacted the art world, influencing various modern movements, including Abstract Expressionism and Minimalism.

After the Russian Revolution in 1917, Malevich actively engaged with the new Soviet government's art policies. He worked as an educator at the Vitebsk Art School, collaborating with artists like El Lissitzky to develop innovative art education programs. However, as the Soviet regime tightened its political control, by the late 1920s, Malevich's abstract art faced increasing criticism.

In the early 1930s, under pressure from the Soviet government, Malevich abandoned abstract art and returned to figurative painting, focusing on portraits and landscapes. He died of cancer on May 15, 1935, in Leningrad (now Saint Petersburg), and famously adorned his coffin with a black square and a circle.

DIE MALERISCHE NATURVERÄNDERUNG UNTER DEM EINFLUSSE DES ERGÄNZUNGSELEMENTS.

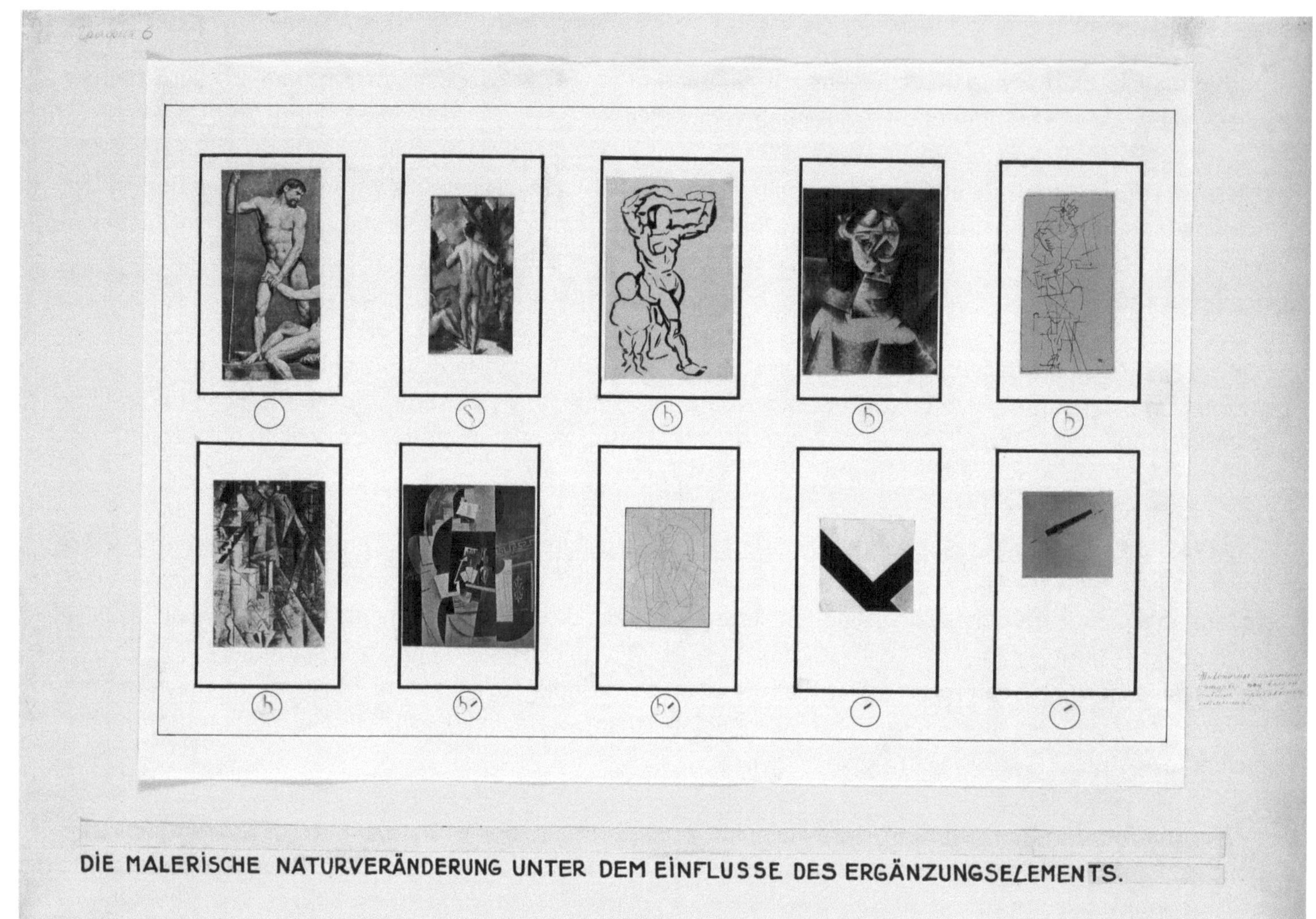

72.4 x 98.4 cm

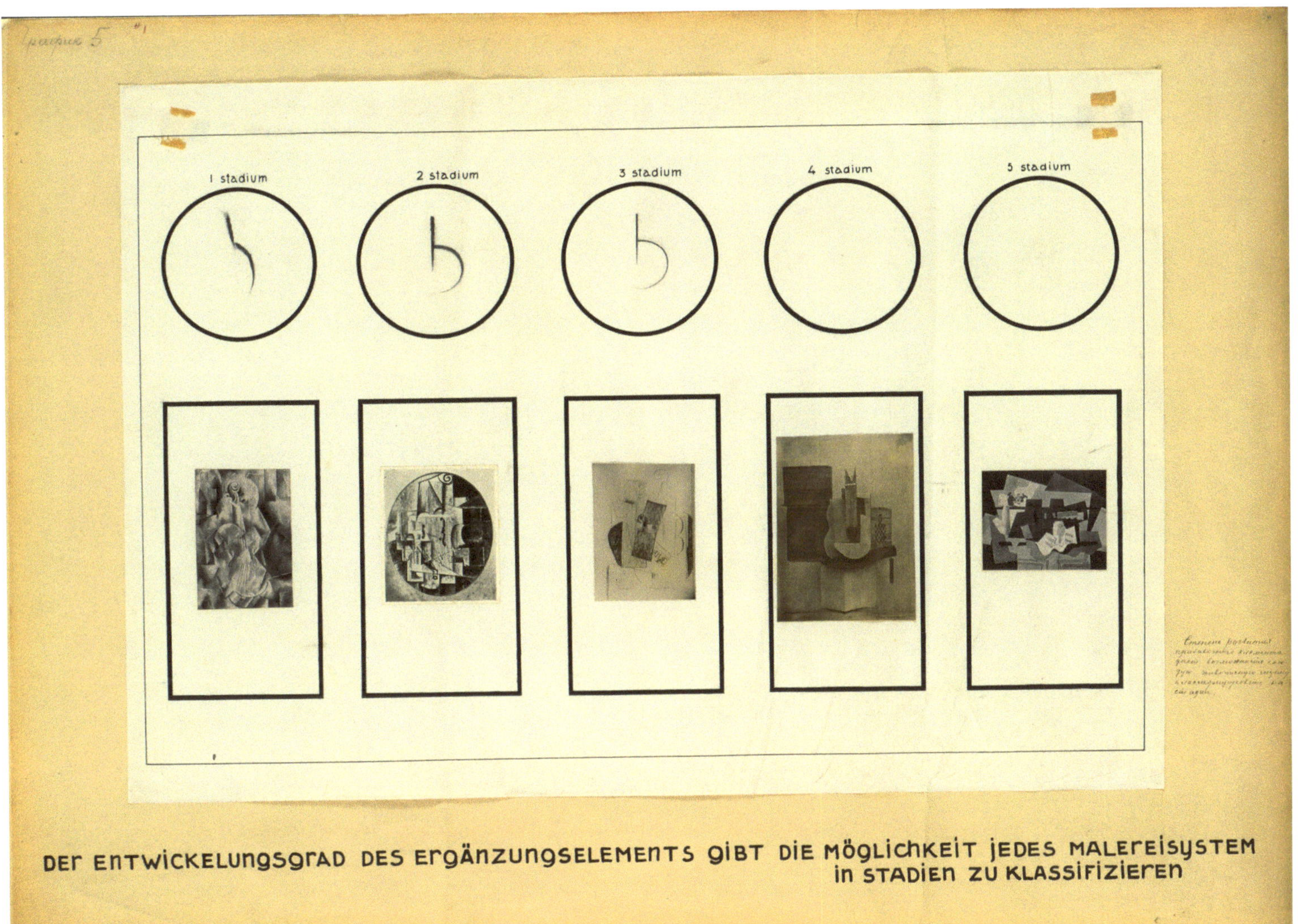
1 stadium
2 stadium
3 stadium
4 stadium
5 stadium
DER ENTWICKELUNGSGRAD DES ERGÄNZUNGSELEMENTS GIBT DIE MÖGLICHKEIT JEDES MALEREISYSTEM
IN STADIEN ZU KLASSIFIZIEREN

Suprematist Elements Squares, 1927

Kurt Schwitters, 1887~1948

Kurt Schwitters was a German painter, sculptor, graphic designer, and poet, primarily associated with collage and the Dada art movement. His innovative style and diverse artistic activities significantly influenced the history of modern art in the 20th century.

Born on June 20, 1887, in Hannover, Germany, Schwitters began his art studies at the Hannover Art School and later trained at the Royal Academy of Fine Arts in Dresden. His early works were traditional paintings influenced by Impressionism and Post-Impressionism.

After World War I, Germany experienced social and political turmoil, which greatly impacted Schwitters's artistic direction. He became deeply interested in the Dada movement, engaging with Dada artists from Zurich and Berlin. However, he did not fully align with the Dadaists and instead founded his own artistic movement called "Merz." The term "Merz" is derived from a word taken from the Commerzbank, and Schwitters used scraps and everyday objects to create his art. He produced collages, sculptures, and installations, seeking to elevate fragments of daily life into art and break down the boundaries of traditional artistic practices.

In 1937, the Nazi regime labeled Schwitters a degenerate artist, severely restricting his artistic activities. Ultimately, he left Germany for Norway and later fled to England to escape the Nazi invasion. In England, he lived in London and the Lake District, continuing his artistic work. He attempted new Merz constructions during this time and continued to create collages and poetry. Despite his previous acclaim in Germany, Schwitters remained relatively unknown in England and faced financial difficulties.

Kurt Schwitters passed away on January 8, 1948, in Kendal, England. Posthumously, he has been reevaluated as a significant figure who greatly influenced various modern art movements, including Dada, Surrealism, abstract art, and Pop Art.

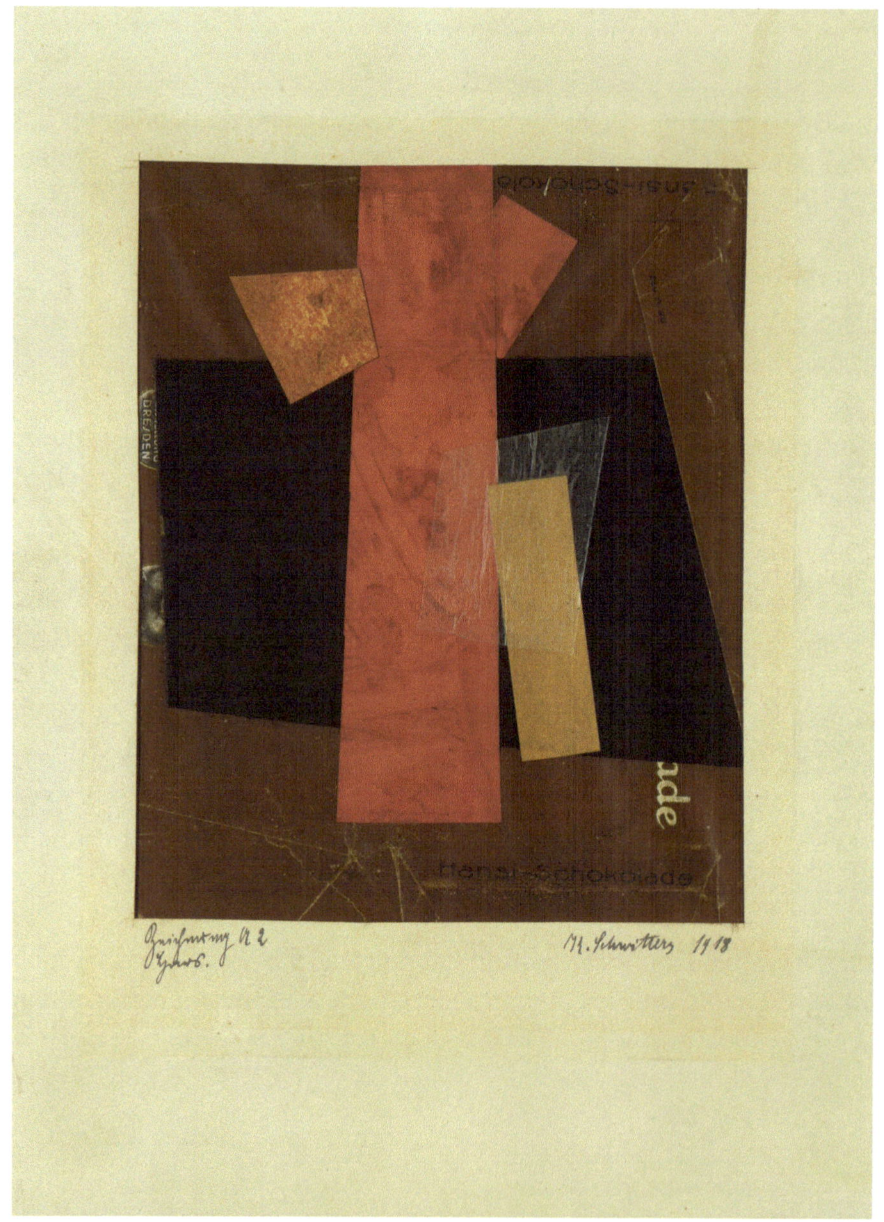

merstoc
ansicht von osten
TZ MEYER & CO. A.G
Kurt Schwitters 1924
Karlsruhe

Gasthöfr
richt u. Rosengarten
such bestens empfohlen.
Bluts
Fahrgeld bezahlt.
F
Ueberfahrt
50 Pfennige
K. Sch. 1920.

·Halbsüß zum
EMERKA

Mz 448
Moskau
K. Schwitters 22.

Mz 252.
K. Schwitters. 1921.
farbige Quadrate.

Kurt Schwitters
eins eins

Relchardt-Schwertschlag
Der Weihnachtsmann

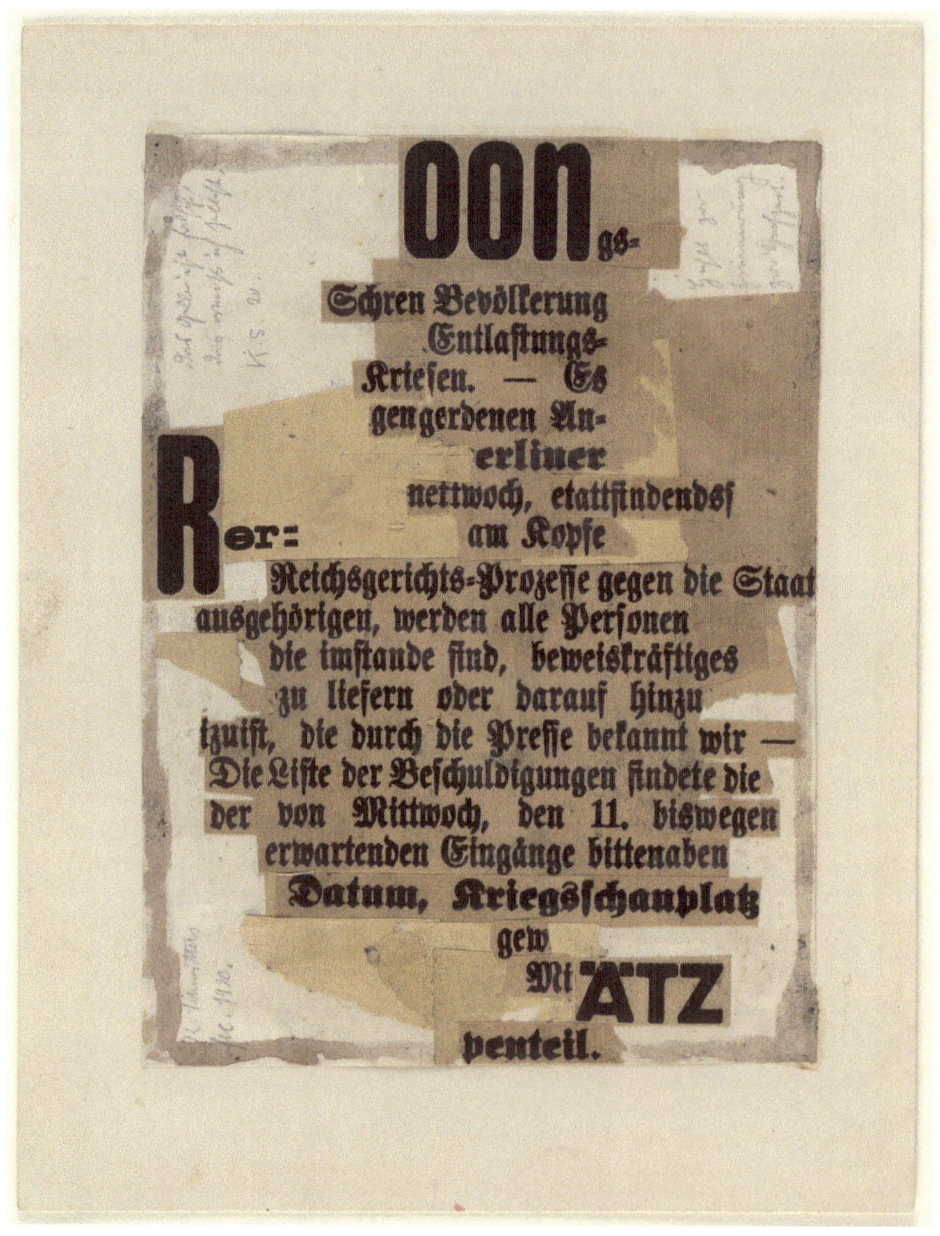
OON gs-
Schren Bevölkerung
Entlastungs-
Kriesen. — Es
gengerdenen An-
erliner
nettwoch, etattfindendsf
R er:
am Kopfe
Reichsgerichts-Prozesse gegen die Staat
ausgehörigen, werden alle Personen
die imstande sind, beweiskräftiges
zu liefern oder darauf hinzu
izuist, die durch die Presse bekannt wir —
Die Liste der Beschuldigungen findete die
der von Mittwoch, den 11. biswegen
erwartenden Eingänge bittenaben
Datum, Kriegsschanplatz
gew
Mi ÄTZ
venteil.

Max Beckmann, 1884~1950

Max Beckmann is a prominent German painter known for his significant role in the Expressionist and New Objectivity (Neue Sachlichkeit) movements. His works are characterized by complex symbolism and intense emotional expression.

Born in Leipzig, Germany, in 1884, Beckmann showed a keen interest in art from a young age. In 1900, he enrolled at the Grand Ducal Art School in Weimar, where he began his formal art education. His 1903 trip to Paris greatly influenced him, and in 1904, he moved to Berlin to pursue his artistic career.

When World War I broke out in 1914, Beckmann volunteered for the medical corps. During the war, he experienced severe psychological and physical trauma, which led him to explore darker themes in his art. After a brief recovery period in 1915 due to the war's trauma, this experience profoundly impacted his artistic vision.

In the 1920s, Beckmann established himself as a key figure in the New Objectivity movement, which sought to move away from the emotional and subjective elements of Expressionism toward more objective and rational depictions of reality. He quickly became a central figure in this movement and was appointed a professor at the Berlin Academy of Arts in 1929. However, with the rise of the Nazi regime in 1933, Beckmann's works were labeled "degenerate art," and he was dismissed from his teaching position. He subsequently emigrated to the Netherlands, where he continued to create art. Despite the difficulties brought on by the Nazi invasion of the Netherlands, he persisted in his artistic output.

In 1947, Beckmann moved to the United States and was appointed a professor at Washington University in St. Louis, where he became active once again. Unfortunately, he passed away suddenly due to a heart attack. His works, which focus on complex symbolism and the human condition amidst chaotic social circumstances, continue to hold an important place in art history worldwide.

A Mirror on an Easel, 1926

50.2 x 64.8 cm

The Chained One, 1944

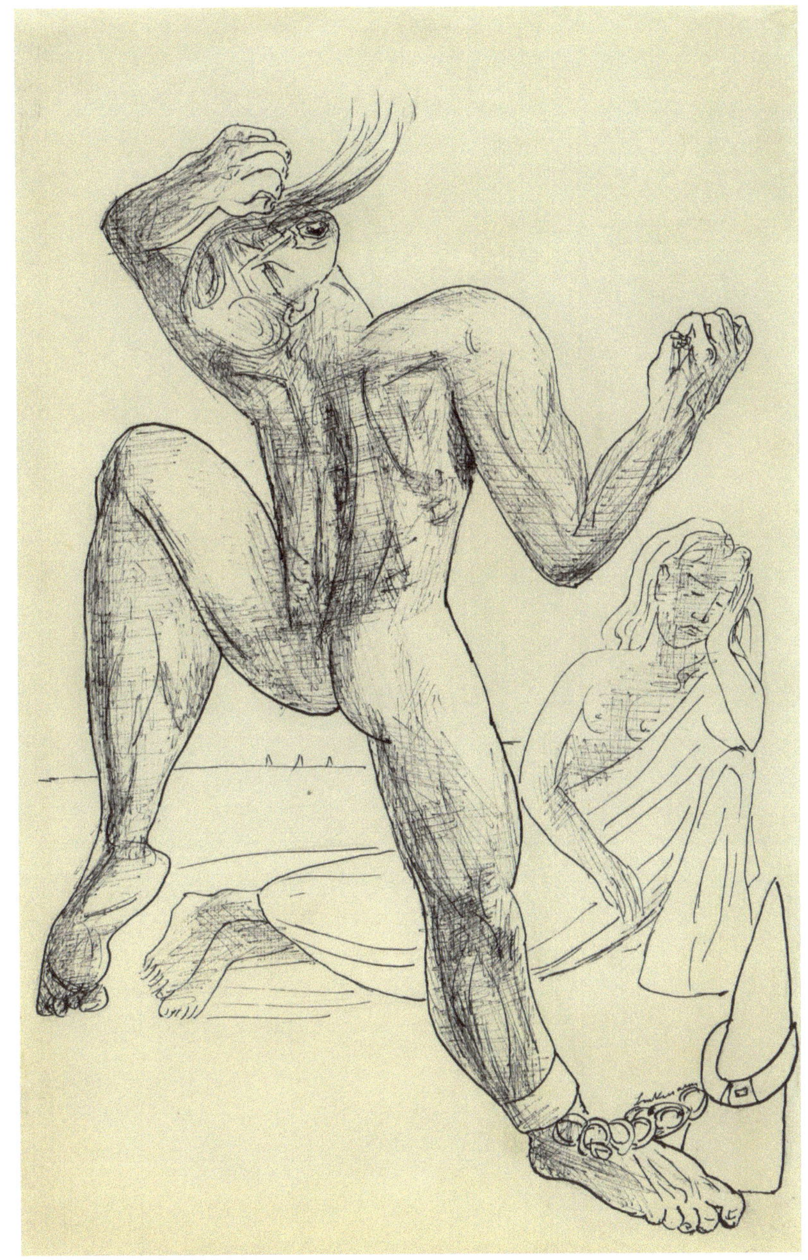

40.3 x 25.4 cm

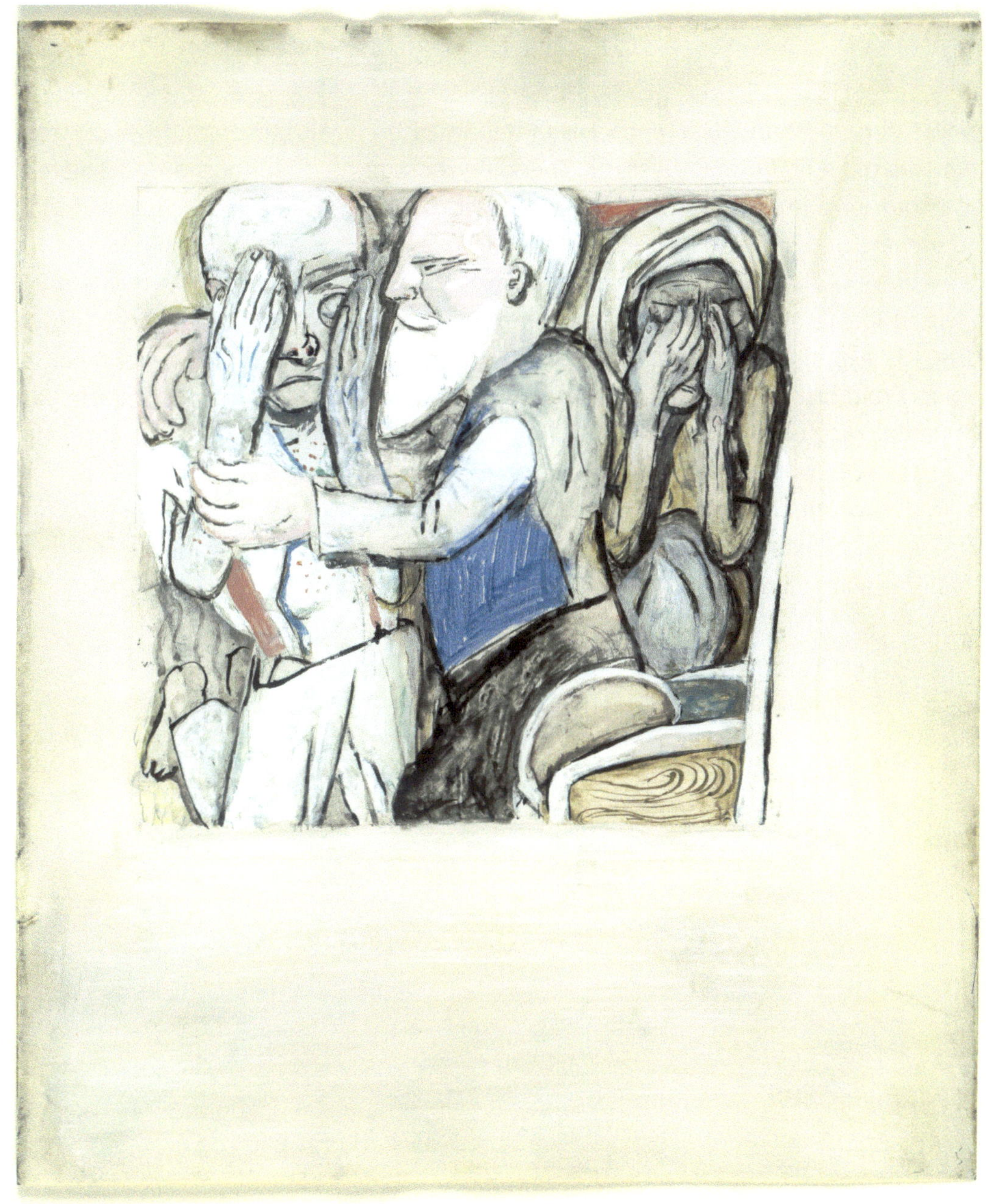

Odilon Redon, 1840~1916

Odilon Redon was born in Bordeaux, France. His father amassed wealth through the slave trade in Louisiana, while his mother was of French Creole descent. Spending most of his childhood on an isolated island, Redon was inspired to explore his imagination and, due to health issues, spent a lot of time alone delving into his inner world and dreams.

Redon is renowned for his symbolist works that embody a unique beauty, particularly known for his use of black in painting. His experiences during the Franco-Prussian War (1870-71) influenced him deeply, and he reflected the horrors and brutality of war in his art. Following this period, he moved to Paris, where he created works and prints employing black.

In the 1890s, Redon produced more vibrant and fantastical works using color and pastels, showcasing mythological figures and Eastern elements. His art is recognized for its religious and mythological themes, along with surrealist elements, marking significant artistic progress.

Christ on the Cross, c.1892

Eye-Balloon, 1878

42.2 x 33.3 cm

Imaginary Figure, c.1881

35.6 x 33 cm

42.5 x 29.5 cm

Winged Horseman, c.1875

40.6 x 26.2 cm

Paul Cézanne, 1839~1906

Paul Cézanne, often referred to as the father of modern art, was born on January 19, 1839, in Aix-en-Provence, France, as the illegitimate child of a wealthy banker.

In 1858, Cézanne began his artistic journey by studying art in Bern, Switzerland. He sought to find his own unique use of color, moving beyond traditional painting techniques. In Paris, he worked at Charles Gleyre's studio, where he developed new painting methods alongside fellow artists like Edgar Degas and Claude Monet. Cézanne aimed to express simultaneous perspectives of nature's diverse planes and angles, continuously exploring his artistic identity. He was deeply inspired by Georges Seurat's pointillism, which he introduced into his own works, simplifying the harmony of color and light while researching ways to express compositional elements. Despite facing rejection at the Paris Salon, he participated in the Salon des Refusés, where he exhibited his work alongside other rejected artists, gaining significant attention.

One of the most important figures in Cézanne's life was Émile Zola, a French novelist, critic, and progressive social activist. They shared a childhood and a close friendship, fueled by a common passion for art and literature. Zola's influence is evident in Cézanne's paintings. As a leader of the naturalism movement in literature, Zola's realist approach left a profound impact on Cézanne's art. Both were keenly aware of the changes in modern society and industrialization, reflecting a shared contemplation on the relationship between nature and humanity. However, as time passed, political differences and divergent artistic directions led to their estrangement. Zola took a leftist political stance advocating for social reform, while Cézanne sought innovation in art while balancing preservation and change, emphasizing his unique vision and structure.

Although Cézanne found success as an artist, he faced social isolation and financial difficulties. In such times, he sought solace in Provence, a region in southern France known for its natural beauty and mild climate. He frequently visited this area, painting its landscapes and finding peace of mind. His works solidified his status as a key figure in post-impressionism, capturing the beauty of nature through the changing light of Provence. A notable series reflecting his affection for the region is the Mont Sainte-Victoire (1880s-90s). Cézanne passed away peacefully at his home in Provence on December 5, 1926.

31.7 x 47.5 cm

Paul Gauguin, 1848~1903

Gauguin was born in Paris and grew up in difficult circumstances, facing poverty and his parents' divorce during his childhood. He joined the navy and later worked as a stockbroker, but ultimately chose the path of an artist. In 1874, he made his debut at a group exhibition with Impressionist painters like Édouard Manet and Claude Monet. This exhibition became a significant opportunity in his artistic career, and his work gradually began to attract attention.

In 1888, Gauguin met Vincent van Gogh and Henri de Toulouse-Lautrec in Paris, forming friendships that would have a lasting impact on his artistic development. His friendship with Van Gogh, in particular, greatly influenced him; Van Gogh's emotional expression and unique use of color inspired Gauguin, while Gauguin's surrealistic approach offered a new perspective to Van Gogh's work. These two artists encouraged each other toward artistic advancement, paving the way for innovation.

After 1888, Gauguin traveled to Tahiti and other Pacific islands, deeply observing the lives of the indigenous people. In June 1891, he arrived at the port of Papeete in Tahiti. Seeking to escape the industrialized Western civilization and pursue art through simple and pure nature, Gauguin faced unexpected challenges in cultural understanding and artistic constraints in Papeete. Ultimately, he moved to Mataiea, where he could freely continue his artistic activities in a more stable environment.

His experiences in Tahiti infused his work with feelings of primitive and natural life, deeply reflecting the pure and simple nature he had longed for since childhood. The lessons he learned in Tahiti provided him with eternal artistic inspiration, playing a crucial role in pioneering a new dimension in his artistic journey. Although Gauguin chose to live in Tahiti, he did not achieve significant commercial success, and his family conflicts deepened during his time on the island, leading to an irreparable rift in their relationship.

Struggling with prolonged illness and substance addiction, he passed away on May 8, 1903. His work only began to receive true recognition after his death and is now held as important collections in galleries and museums worldwide. Gauguin’s art continues to convey the pain and beauty of his experiences and his unique artistic vision to this day.

Museum of Modern Art, New York, USA

Pierre Bonnard, 1867~1947

Pierre Bonnard was a French painter, graphic designer, and literary figure. He is regarded as an important figure in Post-Impressionism, known primarily for his painting style that emphasizes color and the effects of light. He is particularly recognized for his exceptional depictions of interior decoration.

Born on October 3, 1867, in Fontenay-aux-Roses, near Paris, he began studying art at the École des Beaux-Arts in Paris in 1891, where he met fellow artists such as Maurice Denis, Paul Ranson, Paul Sérusier, and Édouard Vuillard. Together, they worked as part of the emerging Impressionist movement and formed a group often referred to as the "Second Impressionism." In 1888, he joined the "Nabis" group, which was led by Maurice Denis and Paul Sérusier. This group aimed to advance modern art based on symbolism and Impressionism, emphasizing new colors and the effects of light while valuing the sensual representation of nature, which greatly influenced Bonnard's work.

Pierre Bonnard is primarily known for his themes of interior scenes and women, delicately expressing the natural changes of light and color. He sought to abstract the forms of objects and convey emotional experiences through harmony in color and light. Focusing on everyday subjects, he frequently painted interior scenes featuring his wife, Marthe. Over time, Bonnard's work became increasingly free, incorporating more personal and emotional elements. He also had a keen interest in literature, engaging in creative writing as a poet.

Robert Delaunay, 1885~1941

Robert Delaunay was born on April 12, 1885, in Paris, France. He is recognized as an important pioneer of modern abstract art and one of the key figures of the New Simultaneism movement. Through his work, Delaunay developed theories of simultaneity and color, which later played a significant role in the development of Post-Impressionism and abstract art.

He became a central figure in the Section d'Or (Golden Section) movement, where he interacted with major contemporary artists like Picasso and Georges Braque, contributing significantly to the advancement of modern art.

Delaunay was known for his bold use of color, developing techniques that freely handled depth, tone, and perspective. He drew inspiration from Paul Cézanne's works, deeply exploring color and volume. Over time, his innovative use of color and geometric forms became comparable to that of Paul Klee. He focused on geometric abstraction, developing a refined and original visual language through simplified forms and vibrant colors.

From 1904 until the First World War, Delaunay showcased his works at the Salon des Indépendants, and in 1906, he was also introduced at the Salon d'Automne in Paris. Through these exhibitions, he established his position within the French art scene. Delaunay was a member of the Nabi group, which aimed to advance modern art based on symbolism and Impressionism. He produced works that focused on urban landscapes and geometric forms, emphasizing the concepts of color and simultaneity. Additionally, through collaboration with his wife Sonia Delaunay, he contributed to textile design and fashion. Together, they showcased modern and innovative fashion and fabric designs utilizing the principles of simultaneity and color.

62.2 x 47 cm

Museum of Modern Art, New York, USA

The Tower, 1911

1910

Suzanne Valadon, 1865~1938

Suzanne Valadon was born on September 23, 1865, as the illegitimate daughter of a poor laundress in Bessines-sur-Gartempe, France. Growing up in a difficult family environment, she began helping with her parents' laundry from the age of six. In her childhood, she worked as an acrobat in a circus but suffered a severe injury after falling from the trapeze, which ended her acrobatic career. After her injury, she took on various jobs and eventually became a housekeeper for the painter Pierre Puvis de Chavannes. It was during this time that she caught his eye and began modeling for him, which led her to realize her hidden artistic talents. While working as a model, she naturally learned the methods of painting from the artists around her. Though she never received formal art education, she honed her skills through this experience and began creating her own unique works.

In 1883, she met Henri de Toulouse-Lautrec, and this marked the beginning of her serious pursuit of painting. They were romantically involved, but the relationship ended after she attempted suicide in 1888. Afterward, Suzanne Valadon gave birth to a child, though the identity of the child's father remains unclear. Several famous painters at the time, including Puvis de Chavannes, Edgar Degas, and Pierre-Auguste Renoir, were speculated to be the father, but all denied the relationship.

Valadon primarily focused on female subjects, especially nudes, presenting a perspective that contrasted with contemporary social norms. Her works, particularly those depicting aging bodies with realism, led to a freer and more direct expression, making a significant impact on the art world by portraying less idealized forms of women.

Suzanne Valadon passed away on April 7, 1938, in Paris. As a bohemian painter who received no formal art training, she was noted for not being bound by any artistic traditions and stood out as a rare female artist of her time.

Drawing for the drypoint Children's Bath in the Garden

Theo van Doesburg, 1883~1931

Theo van Doesburg was born on August 30, 1883, in Utrecht, Netherlands, and was a painter, writer, and architect, known as one of the founders of the De Stijl movement.

In the early 1900s, he studied at the Hague Art Academy, initially influenced by Impressionism and Naturalism before gradually shifting his interest to Expressionism and avant-garde art.

In 1917, van Doesburg, along with Piet Mondrian, Bart van der Leck, and Gerrit Rietveld, started the De Stijl movement. This movement was a visual arts movement formed by Dutch painters, sculptors, and architects that emphasized pure abstract art and geometric forms, primarily using the basic colors of red, blue, and yellow, while also highlighting black and white. The later developed theory of Neo-Plasticism became the core philosophy of the De Stijl movement, emphasizing pure abstraction, geometric forms, and the use of basic colors along with black and white, significantly influencing modern art and design.

Van Doesburg introduced innovative ideas in architecture, working not only in the Netherlands but also in Germany and France. One of his most famous architectural works is the Schröder House in Utrecht, Netherlands. Completed in 1924 in collaboration with Dutch furniture designer and architect Gerrit Rietveld, this house is considered a perfect example of the implementation of De Stijl principles.

In the late 1920s, van Doesburg connected with the Bauhaus art school founded at the Bauhaus University in Germany, engaging with various international artists and designers. However, he faced conflicts with Mondrian due to differences in opinions within the De Stijl movement. Both Piet Mondrian and van Doesburg were key figures in Neo-Plasticism and the De Stijl movement, playing important roles in the development of abstract art, yet their approaches and artistic visions differed. Mondrian adhered to straight lines and right angles, using vertical and horizontal lines along with basic colors to pursue pure abstraction, with his works known for their clarity and precision. In contrast, van Doesburg deviated from Mondrian's strict rules, employing a wider variety of geometric forms and diagonals. He sought to integrate art, architecture, and design into a comprehensive art form.

Philosophically, they also differed. While Mondrian believed that art should aim for a pure form capable of leading social transformation, van Doesburg emphasized the functionality of art and sought art that was closely connected to everyday life. Eventually, when van Doesburg began using diagonals, conflicts arose between the two. Mondrian saw this as a violation of the principles of Neo-Plasticism, leading van Doesburg to leave the De Stijl movement in 1924.

Study for a Composition

10.5 x 14.5 cm

Museum of Modern Art, New York, USA

Théo Van Rysselberghe, 1862~1926

Théo Van Rysselberghe was born on November 23, 1862, into a bourgeois family in Ghent, Belgium. Initially, he followed a traditional academic style in his work but gradually became interested in innovative art movements.

From the early 1880s, influenced by Impressionism, he became a founding member of the Brussels art group Les XX in 1883, where he interacted with innovative artists. Through this group, he came into contact with the French pointillist painter Georges Seurat and became fascinated by pointillism.

In the early 1900s, Van Rysselberghe's painting technique evolved from pointillism to a freer style. He expressed color and form through light and fluid brushstrokes, and the themes of his works became increasingly diverse. His later works are recognized for their unique style, combining elements of Impressionism and Neo-Impressionism. Van Rysselberghe exhibited internationally in France, the Netherlands, and Germany. From 1911, he settled in Saint-Clair, France, where he painted landscapes and portraits of the Mediterranean coast.

Self-Portrait, 1888-89

34 x 25.7 cm

Museum of Modern Art, New York, USA

Umberto Boccioni, 1882~1916

Umberto Boccioni was an Italian painter and sculptor, a key figure in the Italian Futurism movement, which celebrated the dynamism of modern life and the allure of machinery. Born in 1882 in Reggio Calabria, he studied art at the Accademia di Belle Arti in Rome during his youth and later moved to Milan, where he met other artists who shared his interest in Futurist ideas.

Initially influenced by Impressionism and Post-Impressionism, Boccioni soon began to reflect his relentless exploration of speed, technology, and machinery in his work. Through his paintings and sculptures, he abstractly represented elements of modern life, such as trains, factories, and crowds, striving to capture the energy and excitement of contemporary life. He emphasized the Futurist philosophy of technology and progress, believing that societal change and advancement could be achieved through technological development, and asserted that art had the power to lead such transformations. His works aimed to encourage people to embrace a new world and the potential for improving the future.

Tragically, Boccioni's life was cut short when he died in an accident during military training in 1916 at the young age of 33. Despite his early death, his works continue to be celebrated. Boccioni's bold and innovative approach has greatly influenced later artists, and his contributions hold an important place in art history.

Museum of Modern Art, New York, USA

Museum of Modern Art, New York, USA